ADVANCE

BOLDLY GO WHERE NO MAN HAS GONE BEFORE

CHAD GONZALES

Scripture quotations taken from the New King James Version. (NKJV) Copyright © 1982 by Thomas Nelson, Inc. Used by permission. All rights reserved.

Scripture quotations taken from the Amplified® Bible, (AMPC) Copyright © 1954, 1958, 1962, 1964, 1965, 1987 by The Lockman Foundation. Used by permission." (www.Lockman.org)

"Scripture quotations taken from the Amplified® Bible (AMP), Copyright © 2015 by The Lockman Foundation. Used by permission. www.lockman.org"

ISBN: 978-1-7354232-8-9

Copyright © 2024 by Chad Gonzales

www.ChadGonzales.com

All rights reserved.

No part of this book may be reproduced in any form or by any electronic or mechanical means, including information storage and retrieval systems, without written permission from the author, except for the use of brief quotations in a book review.

CONTENTS

Foreword	vii
Introduction	xi
1. Never Settle	1
2. Greater Is Always Possible	11
3. Greater Works Are For Today	21
4. Advance Or Die	29
5. The Fear Of Losing	35
6. The World Is Depending On You	47
7. Storms And Pharisees	51
8. Protect The Dream	65
9. Harness Your Imagination	73
About the Author	81
Also by Chad Gonzales	83
The Supernatural Life Podcast	85
The Healing Academy	87
More from CGM	89
Notes	91

DEDICATION

I dedicate this book to my amazing partners. Without you, none of what we have accomplished and will accomplish is possible. In the worst trial of my life, you were there for me, praying for me, supporting me and encouraging me to keep pushing and keep advancing.

Together, we will go further than any man or woman in Christ has gone before. We will unleash all the glory and authority of Heaven on earth, make satan regret touching us and bring Christ back for His Church.

For eternity, I will forever be grateful for your encouragement and support.

FOREWORD

What a privilege it is for me to introduce you to my friend, Chad Gonzales, and to this great book, *Advance: Boldly Go Where No Man Has Gone Before*. The title alone tells you everything you need to know: There is something you must do in this life! God created each and every one of us to advance—always increasing, always moving forward. We are not meant to retreat or backup or shrink back in any way, shape, or form. As you read this book, you'll be stirred up like never before to keep moving forward, to never settle, and to fulfill with passion everything God has called you to do.

Chad pulls no punches here, and I admire his boldness and transparency throughout. He tells you that you're not going to go through life without challenges, but he offers the answer and solution, which is Jesus and to ADVANCE. Chad holds nothing back and tells you right up front about his own personal life-changing experience with the home going of his first wife, Lacy. That's not an easy thing to go through, but I appreciate his candor and how he's using it as a catalyst and driving force in his life and ministry, which I believe will do the same for you too, no matter what challenge you may be facing.

From cover to cover, I found myself nodding in agreement, as it spoke to the visionary in me. There are so many things I enjoyed in this book, I could spend days talking about them all. I especially liked the chapters "Greater Works Are for Today"; "Protect the Dream"; and "Harness Your Imagination". You'll find that Chad pays special attention to John 14:12 throughout this book, and it's one that I personally love. A lot of people read that verse and totally miss it. They say, "Well, that was just for Jesus." No, actually, it's not.

That is Jesus talking to you and me, and it's a command for all of us who believe. I also agree with Chad wholeheartedly that you must protect the dream that God has given you (believe the Word God has given you about it, guard it, and don't make excuses for it); as well as how your imagination is vital to seeing the fulfillment of your dream. Imagination is actually a form of faith. And if you really want to understand how faith works, watch a child when they begin to imagine things and when they play. One moment they are riding around with a little car on the floor, and before you know it, in their mind, they're inside that car.

Well, that's telling me that you can go where no man has gone before!

There is vision in every page, and each chapter is pregnant with revelation that will lead you to advance in every area of your life. This book will bring you to another level in your spiritual, natural, and financial thinking. You'll begin to experience and see things in the physical realm that you've been praying for in the spiritual realm. You will take hold of things in the faith realm and bring them into the physical realm. Watch for it, because it's going to start happening immediately. Believe it, receive it, and expect it today.

So, Chad, thank you for allowing me to be a part of this book. And to those of you reading this: I guarantee that if you'll believe it, it will change your life. And I'm not talking about when you get to Heaven; I mean right here, right now! You can possess what you want here in this life—and when you get to Heaven, you can be one of the teachers instead of one of the students!

Friend, this is more than just a book. If you will accept what it says, it will become a living reality that will always cause you to excel and move forward in life. Enjoy this good read, as I did. It's one you'll want to go back to and revisit, and it's one you'll want to share with others. You will find that this directive to advance is something you simply cannot do without.

Dr. Jesse Duplantis

Evangelist, Author, TV Host; President and Founder of Jesse Duplantis Ministries

INTRODUCTION

In a world constantly evolving with innovation and technology, the Church seems stalled, with diminished echoes of divine miracles. Are we merely seeking a revival of past spiritual triumphs, or aiming to unlock unprecedented realms of divine glory never seen before?

The Church has lingered in a cycle of familiarity, adhering to past spiritual vibrancy. A divine call urges believers to surpass previous boundaries, embrace audacity, manifest extraordinary wonders, and radiate heavenly glory. Heaven seeks those ready to forge unparalleled paths of divine power and revelation, marking not just a revival but a new era.

Our journey isn't devoid of challenges; it's punctuated with battles, adversities, and divine orchestrations. Such was the battle I faced with the transition of my first wife, Lacy, to heaven.

THE ENEMY FIRES

In the fierce battleground of spiritual warfare, I stood as a formidable threat to the realms of darkness, armored in unwavering faith. Our ministry was advancing to a realm where divine healings were taking place and the impossible became testimonies of miracles - tumors disappeared, blind eyes were seeing, and the lame were skipping and running around sanctuaries.

Lacy's ascent to Heaven wasn't merely a passage but a cold, calculated assault designed to demolish our ministry's momentum. Satan had a sinister plot against us and aimed his artillery at me, seeking to obliterate the growing wave of miracles and divine revelations illuminating our path. As a gateway to divine truths, my book, "The Supernatural Prayer of Jesus," was scheduled to release just two days from her passing; a time table that seethed cruel intention.

As brutal as the injury was, it would be a poignant reminder that adversities aren't merely obstacles; if we allow them, they can be divine catalysts propelling us into realms of victory, authority, and unparalleled spiritual manifestations.

THE SEED OF A DREAM

The night after Lacy passed, I had a dream. In the dream, I found myself walking down a path outside. In the distance, about 200 feet away, I saw a lion. It hadn't seen me yet. I got very still and started to back up and then it turned its head slightly and saw me. The lion began walking to its right, went past a tree and started circling around to my right.

I started jumping up and down, waving my arms and screaming, trying to make myself appear larger, but the lion began to run towards me. I then began to run at the lion full speed. When I got close to the lion, it stood up on its hind legs and turned into a man with a lion costume on He took off running away from me, tripped and hit his head on a rock. His head split halfway open and he was bleeding out. I walked up to him and said, "You might want to call 911" and walked away.

When I woke up, I immediately had two scriptures come to my mind:

1 Peter 5:8 NKJV
Be sober, be vigilant; because your adversary the devil walks about like a roaring lion, seeking whom he may devour.

James 4:7 NKJV
Therefore submit to God. Resist the devil and he will flee from you.

I knew this was a God dream; He was showing me not only was this an attack of the devil, but also I was spiritually in the right position - I was ready.

We are always on offense and we never retreat. Never. Never. Never. Instead of retreating, we advance.

Never run from a lion...especially a fake one. Instead, become the lion and advance after your enemy.

PROVOKED TO ADVANCE

As I was on my return flight from a conference in California, just weeks after Lacy's passing, I found myself rewatching the movie *Braveheart,* a cinematic masterpiece starring Mel Gibson. Gibson, embodying the essence of a fearless warrior, donned a rustic kilt, unruly long hair, and rugged leather armor. He portrayed Sir William Wallace, a formidable Scottish knight who rose as a pivotal leader during the trying times of the First War of Scottish Independence in the late 1200s.

The movie unveils a heart-wrenching moment that fuels Wallace's rebellion. His beloved wife, an irreplaceable part of his soul, was brutally captured and murdered in the town square. This vile act, executed before a crowd of onlookers, was a malicious ploy. The English endeavored to shatter Wallace's spirit, seizing what was most dear to him to force his submission and quash his spirit of defiance.

But they miscalculated. Instead of diminishing his resolve, the cruel loss of his wife ignited a roaring fire within Wallace. It steeled his determination, compelling him to champion the cause of Scottish independence with unwavering valor and an unyielding thirst for justice against his adversaries.

A vivid scene from the movie sears the mind - Wallace, face boldly adorned with strokes of white and blue paint, mounts his horse, standing defiantly before his battalion of loyal men. With the poise of a true leader and the heart of a lion, he delivers a rousing speech that echoes through the highlands: "They may take our lives, but they will never take our freedom!" This passionate declaration crystallized his unyielding spirit and the unwavering courage of his men in the face of adversity.

Braveheart had long been a film that resonated with me, but on that flight back home, with the wound of Lacy's passing still raw, my connection to it deepened in a powerful way. As I watched, the story of William Wallace took on a new, personal dimension. His pain, his rage, his unyielding quest for freedom—I felt them as my own. In that reflective altitude, amidst the clouds, the Holy Spirit spoke to me about our future and the Advance conferences that lay on the horizon. I was guided to re-envision our ministry's symbol; to adorn our lion's face with the iconic white and blue paint of Braveheart's warrior. It was more than a logo—it was a banner under which we would march forward, embodying the spirit of Wallace's relentless fight and his unwavering will for freedom.

When I look at our Advance logo, I don't see just a picture; I see a mission. I was already on a mission, but after the attack of satan against my family, it poured a tanker of gasoline on the fire that was already burning within me. Instead of retreating, it just ticked me off and pushed me even harder to advance further with more vigilance, more determination and more intentionality according to His power that works in me mightily.

Satan wanted me to stop me; he wanted me to quit. But when satan took Lacy, he inadvertently took away any possible 'quit' I had in me. I live in joy but also with a controlled anger that I allow to stay present just below the surface. None will know the hurt that's behind my smile, but all will know the power of God fueled by the fire of justice.

Every day I will grow. Every day I will advance. Every day I will increase. Every day I will multiply. I will not stop. Never.

Bring on the critics...they simply push me. Bring on the naysayers...they simply add more fuel to the fire.

I advance out of revenge for Lacy. I advance out of devotion to my Lord. I advance for the sake of the world. I advance to destroy the works of darkness. I advance to show the Church what is possible in Christ.

Friend, I invite you to advance with me. Let's make the choice to never settle for average, but boldly go where no believer has ever gone before.

CHAPTER 1
NEVER SETTLE

In the science fiction television series *Star Trek*, each episode started with a speech by Captain Kirk, in which he said, "Space: the final frontier. These are the voyages of the starship *Enterprise*. Its five-year mission: to explore strange new worlds; to seek out new life and new civilizations; to boldly go where no man has gone before!" This last phrase, "…To go boldly where no man has gone before…" really is at the heart of every individual, whether they realize it or not. At the core of all humanity is a spiritual foundation; we are spirit beings living in a body. Innately, we know there is more to this world than what we experience with our five senses; we may not recognize it, but it is the piece that drives humanity to explore and push the limits and boundaries around us.

When you look at the history of mankind, we see a constant push for advancement. Wars continued for centuries as nations engaged in conquest to advance their territories. Explorers like Christopher Columbus and Ferdinand Magellan challenged the prevailing beliefs about what was possible in exploring new lands and routes around the world. We can look at scientists such as George Washington Carver, who credited his times of prayer with God, in finding over three hundred products from peanuts and Thomas Edison, whose inventions radically changed the world.

We find people such as Chuck Yeager, who was willing to put his life on the line to break the sound barrier, which people said was impossible. At the time, many feared that supersonic flight was impossible because of an invisible "barrier" that could destroy aircraft. As Yeager later stated, "I realized that the mission had to end in a let-down because the real barrier wasn't in the sky but in our knowledge and experience of supersonic flight."

I look around at all of the different educational, business and technological organizations and institutions; within them, you see a constant and continual push for advancement and growth. The businesses and institutions that push for growth, they almost always advance; the ones that settle for where they are at, they begin to fall behind and many eventually fade away.

I then look at the Church and ask, "Where is the advancement?" "Where is the push for growth?" Throughout Church history, we see an extreme minority of individuals, that at various times, have pushed to go where no one has gone before. In the secular world, we can find scores of examples of individuals who have pushed past normal and advanced. In the Church world, it's so rare to find people that have advanced, our list of Church heroes over a thousand years pales in comparison to the secular advances of the last century.

Last year, the Lord said this to me during a time of study: "Always advancing. Always increasing. Always multiplying." I have never been satisfied with staying stagnant, but this statement has been a fire in me and driving me even more. God wants growth!

Not only does God want growth, the world needs growth from the Church. The Church should not be looking to the world for ideas. The church folk are the ones filled with the Revealer of Truth! A Christian has the Genius of the universe living on the inside of them. We are told in 1 Corinthians 14:2 that we can pray out the deep, secret, mysterious things of God! People filled with God should be leading the way in the advancement of all areas of life; unfortunately, too many Christians have relegated God to the church on Sunday instead of life on Monday. Thankfully, we have some Christian leaders who are starting to wake up to what can happen when you allow God to bring revelation and wisdom to each area of our lives.

During Covid, the Church world was crying "You can't close us down because we are essential." Well, the world didn't care because they didn't see the Church as essential. Do you know why? You are only essential if you have something the other doesn't. The world was looking for a cure and all the Church could do was pass out gift cards and food. The Church turned into a social service organization instead of a supernatural organization. How can you be essential when you are looking to the world's systems as your source? Certainly people need Jesus, but let me ask you an honest question: When you look at the lives of the average Christian, is it really any different than the lives of the sinners?

As a whole, the Church world has been stuck in a rut for quite some time. Yes, I know the Church is quietly growing throughout the world. I have friends all over the world who are doing remarkable things for God and radically changing nations, but as a whole, we are in the same place in our revelation and understanding of things. We are still looking back and talking about the good old days and of the miracles that took place in the 1900s instead of telling of the miracles that took place last week. Thank God for those that blazed trails before us, but we shouldn't be just talking about their miracles - we should be talking about our own!

Friend, it is time for us to advance. It is time for us to go after greater and I for one am determined that not only will I not stay the same, but I will be one to help lead the charge to go further than anyone has gone before in the things of God. Jesus expected greater, so we should expect greater.

We should have a burning on the inside that we will not stay put, but that we will go further. We will not camp out on the foundation of those before us, but we will build upon it!

I refuse to dishonor those who have blazed trails for me by simply building a camp at the end of their trail. The greatest way I can show honor to those I truly honor is to pick up the torch and press forward at all costs to go further than what man has done before. Why? Because (1) Jesus said it was possible and (2) Jesus expects it.

I don't care how impossible it looks, it is always possible. God specializes in making the impossible possible and yet He created us to be just like Him. Jesus said in Matthew 19:26, "With man, this is impossible, but with God, all things are possible." He went on to say in Mark 9:23, "If you can believe, all things are possible to him who believes." Do you see that? Your faith puts in the God class of operation. Because God is our Father, the impossibilities of this world become our playground! Jesse Duplantis, my spiritual father, says it like this,

"Believe the unbelievable and receive the impossible because it's doable!"

I've never liked it when someone told me, "No." There has always been a little bit of rebel in me. I've certainly never liked it when someone told me that I couldn't accomplish something. I have always been the type that if you tell me that, you automatically go on my list: my list of those that I will set out the rest of my life, endeavoring to prove to you that you are wrong.

I dealt with it even as a kid. As a freshman in high school, I was playing football and basketball. I was really good in football because of my build and my speed, but I loved basketball…even though I wasn't that good. One day in football practice, the head varsity coach called me out in front of everyone and said, "Gonzales, why don't you quit basketball. You have a great shot of playing some big time college football, but you'll never do anything with basketball because you suck at it." Well, that just ticked me off. I took off my helmet, walked off the field, turned in my football equipment and quit. Why? I was going to prove him wrong. The biggest hurdle? I wasn't that great at basketball and I wasn't tall.

During my freshman basketball season, things didn't go well - most of my time during games was spent sitting on the bench! However, that spring and summer, I worked - hard! Almost every day, I was at the track running in my strength shoes, lifting weights and working on my basketball skills. Do you know what happened my sophomore year? I was a starter on the JV squad and a few weeks into the season, I was bumped up to the varsity squad. In one year, I went from riding the bench to playing on the varsity team. Over the next two years, I continued to work, not only for myself but also to prove that football coach wrong. I continued to get better and better until I became the captain of my team and won several awards while playing against some of the best players in the state of Texas and in the US.

At the end of high school, me and one of my teammates ended up going to play at the collegiate level. As a result, our local newspaper did an article on us - and do you know what I did? I cut out the article, went to that football coaches office and I taped it on his door!

When I was a freshman in high school, I remember sitting in English class and my teacher, in front of everyone, said, "Chad, you'll never make it to college." I don't remember what she said before or after that…all I remember was she said I couldn't do it. Well, I told my mom about it and you better believe my mother was at that school chewing that teacher out! I'll never forget sitting in the hallway, with the rest of my class while we listened to my mother give that teacher an earful! But that statement by that teacher put a fire in me. I already had my plans of going to college and things I wanted to accomplish...but she went on my list. It was one of the reasons I pushed myself to not only get my bachelors degree, but to go on and obtain my masters degree and my doctorate.

That same attitude that was in me as a kid and young adult is still in me now as I'm quickly approaching the young age of 50. The drive that pushed me as a kid has now been driving me in ministry for two decades. Don't tell me I can't do something! Don't tell me it's not possible!

I've had ministers tell me that the statements of Jesus aren't for me. I've been told you can't do this and can't do that. They don't realize all they are doing is throwing gasoline on the fire within me. There is a small part of me that hopes when we get to Heaven, Jesus will gather all the naysayers together and and just for one moment, allow me to look at them and say, "I told you I would do it!"

If there are two things that drives me bonkers, it is complaining and excuses. I just can't do either one. I don't like complaining because I believe in maintaining an attitude of gratitude. God is so good and we should be thankful at all times for what God has done and is doing for and through us. I also don't like excuses. Either put up or shut up but don't make excuses. Own your mistakes, own your lack of gumption, own your lack of desire to advance...but don't make excuses for it. Sadly, I often hear excuses for our lack of advancement from many in the Church. The world doesn't put up with excuses; you provide excuses, you get fired. In the Church, we get excuses and find scripture for them so as to make ourselves feel better and not have to push forward. I refuse to make excuses when Jesus has not only provided the way, but also told us it is possible to always hear and see from God, greater and greater and greater — not only for our fellowship but also so the Church and the world can say, "Wow!"

It's time to stop settling and it's time to start advancing.

CHAPTER 2
GREATER IS ALWAYS POSSIBLE

There are a few statements Jesus made that have been the driving force in my life. One is found in John 14:12 in which Jesus said, "Whoever believes in Me will do the same works and even greater works than these He will do because I'm going to the Father." Jesus revealed that what He did on the earth was to be the floor, not the ceiling, for the works of the Church. Jesus expected increase from the Church. Jesus expected that His seating at the right hand of God would be the launching of the Church into an advancement of Himself in the world. Jesus fully expected His Church, His body to partake of all authority in Heaven and on earth, their union with Christ and blow past what Jesus did on the earth with a lesser authority and operating under a lesser covenant. (Matthew 28:18 and Hebrews 8:6-9)

The second statement is found in John 5:20 in which Jesus states, "The Father will show me how to do even greater works than these, just so you will marvel."

There are a number of things I want to point out about Jesus' statement in John 5. First of all, Jesus tells us that He can do nothing without the Father. This statement alone blows holes in people's theology that Jesus did everything He did because He was God. Certainly, Jesus is God; however, Jesus did everything that He did on the earth as a man, not as God. *How do we know this?*

1. Jesus laid aside all of His Godlike abilities, humbled Himself and came to earth as a man.

Philippians 2:6-8 AMP
Who, although being essentially one with God *and* in the form of God but possessing the fullness of the attributes which make God God, did not think this equality with God was a thing to be eagerly grasped *or* retained, But stripped Himself of all privileges and rightful dignity, so as to assume the guise of a servant (slave), in that He became like men *and* was born a human being. And after He had appeared in human form, He abased *and* humbled Himself [still further] and carried His obedience to the extreme of death, even the death of the cross!

2. Jesus was tempted in every way like us - God cannot be tempted.

Hebrews 2:18 AMPC
For because He Himself [in His humanity] has suffered in being tempted (tested and tried), He is able [immediately] to run to the cry of (assist, relieve) those who are being tempted *and* tested *and* tried [and who therefore are being exposed to suffering].

Hebrews 4:15 AMPC
For we do not have a High Priest Who is unable to understand *and* sympathize *and* have a shared feeling with our weaknesses *and* infirmities *and* liability to the assaults of temptation, but One Who has been tempted in every respect as we are, yet without sinning.

James 1:13 AMPC
Let no one say when he is tempted, I am tempted from God; for God is incapable of being tempted by [what is] evil and He Himself tempts no one.

3. Jesus was anointed by God...and God doesn't need to be anointed!

Acts 10:38 AMPC
How God anointed *and* consecrated Jesus of

Nazareth with the [Holy] Spirit and with strength *and* ability *and* power; how He went about doing good and, in particular, curing all who were harassed *and* oppressed by [the power of] the devil, for God was with Him.

4. Jesus was growing in wisdom

Luke 2:40 AMPC
And the Child grew and became strong *in spirit*, filled with wisdom; and the grace (favor and spiritual blessing) of God was upon Him.

John 5:20 AMPC
The Father dearly loves the Son and discloses to (shows) Him everything that He Himself does. And He will disclose to Him (let Him see) greater things yet than these, so that you may marvel *and* be full of wonder *and* astonishment.

Jesus was doing life as a man anointed by God, filled with God and united with God.

I know this is going to be a shocker for many people, but Jesus didn't know everything! Jesus was not walking around Israel as the omniscient all knowing Jesus of Nazareth; Jesus was learning and growing like all of us! Jesus blatantly discloses this when He said, "The Father is going to show me even greater things!"

Jesus makes it extremely clear that He was going to be shown things He did not know.

Not only does Jesus' statement reveal He was doing life as a man, it also reveals His expectancy for growth! I cannot tell you how much I absolutely love the fact the Holy Spirit gave us this truth. Jesus, although the Son of God, was doing life as the Son of Man and not only was growing, but was also expecting growth. Jesus was expecting greater revelation and insight from the Father so He could advance in life and help others advance too! If Jesus was always looking to grow, we should always be looking to grow.

In addition to revealing Jesus' humanity and His hunger for growth, we also see from John 5:19-20 that Jesus was expecting the Father to reveal the realities for the necessary growth. How did Jesus grow in revelation? Jesus grew in revelation through fellowship with the Father. Jesus fully expected the Father to speak to Him and show Him things He had never heard or seen before.

> John 5:19-20 NKJV
> Then Jesus answered and said to them, "Most assuredly, I say to you, the Son can do nothing of Himself, but what He sees the Father do; for whatever He does, the Son also does in like manner. For the Father loves the Son, and shows Him all things that He Himself does; and He will

show Him greater works than these, that you may marvel."

Notice what Jesus said, "I only do the things I see my Father do." This statement shows us that revelation comes through fellowship, not memorization. Too many Christians are expecting to grow in revelation because they memorized scriptures. In Bible days, every Jewish male had to memorize the first five books of the Old Testament; the Pharisees would memorize not only the law, but massive portions of the Old Testament as well. We see how this worked out with the Pharisees! They knew all of the written Scripture but they didn't recognize the Word of God (Jesus) that stood right in front of them! I know many preachers today that know a lot of Scripture, but it's apparent in listening to them that they do not know the Father. Great intellect does not always translate into great revelation. You can be really smart and still be ignorant!

The Bible says in Romans 10:17, "Faith comes by hearing the Word of God." The phrase 'Word of God' in the Greek text is literally the word *Rhema,* which *means* "the spoken word of God."[1] Certainly we need to read our Bibles, but simply reading your Bible doesn't produce revelation and insight - that only comes by the Holy Spirit being your Teacher and Revealer of Truth. When I read my Bible, I don't read for information; I read for revelation! I read with full expectation that the

Holy Spirit to show me things I have never heard before.

You know what? I also expect to get revelation and insight outside of my Bible reading time as well! While I am sitting outside, riding my lawnmower, pushing a shopping cart in a grocery store or even in the shower, I am always endeavoring to be on alert for God's voice. During my times of prayer, I am expecting God to show me something or tell me something I have never seen or heard before. Why? Because God wants growth and Jesus showed me in John 5 that growth is not only possible but an ordinary part of fellowship with God.

You cannot separate fellowship with God from spiritual growth; it is just not possible. I have kept a journal for many years now and my journals are filled with thoughts and insights I have gotten from the Holy Spirit at various times. I expect to hear from Him all of the time; as a result, I take my journal with me everywhere I go. Why? Because when He speaks, I write it down so I don't forget it. If you are not honoring the Word you are given, don't expect for God to cast His pearls before you. If I hear and do nothing with it, I inadvertently count it as worthless and make myself a fool. The wisdom of God is precious and we should not only honor it, but expect to gain more and more every day.

I enjoy going through my older journals at various times - simply to see how much I have grown. However, at the end of each year, I will pull out the prior year's journal and look to see what I have learned and how far I have gone. It is always amazing to me that there are some things I understand now that I had maybe only grasped a year or two ago. One thing I can say is this: I am always growing because I must always be advancing, always increasing and always multiplying; the world needs it and God requires it.

I am always pushing for growth and I can honestly say, every year I am growing in revelation. It's not because I am special; it is because I am hungry. Did you notice that when you are hungry, nothing else matters but finding food? The thought of food consumes you and everything else goes by the wayside. This is the way that revelation must be for you and I…it is our passion and thus our pursuit.

My daily prayer for over two decades has been that God would give me increased revelation and understanding of Him and His ways. This prayer has been based on the apostle Paul's prayers for the Ephesians.

> Ephesians 1:15-23 AMP
> Therefore I also, after I heard of your faith in the Lord Jesus and your love for all the saints, do not cease to give thanks for you, making mention of you in my prayers: that the God of our Lord Jesus Christ, the Father of glory, may give to you the spirit of wisdom and revelation

in the knowledge of Him, the eyes of your understanding being enlightened; that you may know what is the hope of His calling, what are the riches of the glory of His inheritance in the saints, and what *is* the exceeding greatness of His power toward us who believe, according to the working of His mighty power which He worked in Christ when He raised Him from the dead and seated *Him* at His right hand in the heavenly *places,* far above all principality and power and might and dominion, and every name that is named, not only in this age but also in that which is to come. And He put all *things* under His feet, and gave Him *to be* head over all *things* to the church, which is His body, the fullness of Him who fills all in all.

Notice Paul's prayer was not for God to give us possessions but to give us wisdom and revelation in the knowledge of Him. This has been my daily prayer not only for myself, but also my family and my ministry partners. Why do I want increased revelation? Because I know that revelation leads to manifestations, growth and advancement.

The amazing thing about God is: there is always more! If you ever get to the point where you think you have learned all there is to know — you have just shown yourself to be dumb! We will always be growing and advancing in the things of God throughout eternity so why would you think there isn't more available right now!

Jesus told us that greater was available, so why not go after it? If Jesus was pursuing greater, we should be pursuing greater. We should always be advancing because it is possible!

CHAPTER 3
GREATER WORKS ARE FOR TODAY

In John 14:12, Jesus made an astounding statement. He said, "Whoever believes in Me will do the same works and even greater works because I am going to the Father."

This verse captured my attention many years ago and was the fuel that was poured on the fire that had been burning in me since I was twenty years old. When I found out God was real, I made the decision that everything Jesus said in the Bible was possible. When I came across John 14:12, as daunting of a statement as it was, I believed it was possible and doable because Jesus said it.

Let's break this statement down. First of all, Jesus said, "Whoever believes in Me..." This promise was not to the person who stands behind a pulpit. This promise was not to a graduate of a Bible school or someone in full time ministry. This promise was to the believer.

Are you a "whoever?" If you are a believer in Jesus, you qualify. What do you qualify for? You qualify for the promise Jesus made: "Whoever believes in me will do the same works…"

What are the "same works?" Every time Jesus mentioned "doing the works," He was always referring to miracles. When John the Baptist sent his disciples to question Jesus if He truly was the Christ, Jesus didn't respond by talking about all of the social services He had provided nor the large number of people He had following Him.

> Luke 7:20-22 NKJV
> "When the men had come to Him, they said, "John the Baptist has sent us to You, saying, 'Are You the Coming One, or do we look for another?' " And that very hour He cured many of infirmities, afflictions, and evil spirits; and to many blind He gave sight. Jesus answered and said to them, "Go and tell John the things you have seen and heard: that the blind see, the lame walk, the lepers are cleansed, the deaf hear, the dead are raised, the poor have the gospel preached to them."

Whenever questioned about His identity, Jesus consistently referred to signs, wonders, and miracles as validation. Why am I pointing this out? Because even though Jesus said we could do the same works as Him, people have tried to water down what Jesus said.

Some say that Jesus was only talking about us being able to feed the hungry and help the poor. The problem with this belief is that even a demon filled person can do that! There are evil people in the world that help the poor for political reason, tax write offs or to help change their social image.

Other people want to say that Jesus was talking about us doing the same social work because... "We could not do the supernatural works of Jesus because He was God on the earth." Well, we already thoroughly proved in the last chapter that Jesus was doing life as a man — so that belief is debunked too.

Another fact that people do not want to consider is that many of the miracles that Jesus did, had already been accomplished by people such as Moses, Joshua, Elijah and Elisha.

For example, do you realize Jesus was not the first person to multiply food or raise the dead? We find that Elisha multiplied food for over one hundred men. Elijah and Elisha both raised people from the dead. One could dare say that some of the miracles that Moses, Elijah, and Elisha accomplished were actually more spectacular than what Jesus did. Moses parted the Red Sea as well as caused water to come out of a rock on two different occasions; Elijah called fire out of Heaven; both Elijah and Elisha parted the Jordan River and walked across it.

When Jesus sent out the twelve and the seventy (Luke 9; Luke 10), they all came back with reports of people getting healed and delivered of demons…and none of the disciples were saved yet!

Friend, let's take Jesus' words for what they are: true, possible and doable. Jesus meant what He said; we can do what He did. Why would this be possible? Because of salvation! The result of Jesus going to be with the Father was that salvation would be provided and thus, we would be united with Christ, having the same position with God in Christ and the same authority on the earth.

Now, let's get to the final portion of Jesus promise: greater works.

There has been much debate over this last phrase and I truly don't understand why people want to argue and try to come up with excuses for it. In reality, the only reason people want to come up with excuses for it is because they are simply faithless cowards looking for an excuse to hide behind. When Jesus said we could do greater works than what He did on the earth, He literally meant it.

For the minority of Christians who do think miracles are possible, most of those think the 'greater works' of Jesus are simply the Church doing more, numerically, because there would be more of us.

Well, that's better than believing we can't produce the miraculous at all...BUT IT IS NOT WHAT JESUS SAID. Jesus didn't say we would do more frequent works or more widespread works; Jesus said we would do greater works.

With the exception of an extremely small minority of people, that I call the 8 Percent, the rest of Christianity, would say that the works Jesus did on the earth would be the ceiling of what the Church could accomplish. But again, that can't be possible because Jesus said we would do greater.

In reality, the works Jesus did on the earth is not the ceiling for the Church— it is the floor! *The works of Jesus on the earth is the least of what the Church should be doing today.* I know it may sound crazy to the religious mind, but it makes perfect sense to the Heavenly mind.

My friend, it is actually very simple because of four scriptural reasons.

1. Jesus was operating under the Old Covenant.
   Jesus was showing us what was possible as a

man united with God under a limited covenant with limited authority.

2. Jesus was not walking in all the glory that was available. In His supernatural prayer in John 17, Jesus said, "Father, restore unto Me the glory I had before the world began." (John 17:5)
3. Jesus was not walking in all the authority that was available. Only after Jesus took the keys of death, hell, and the grave and arose victorious, did He declare, "All authority in Heaven and Earth is mine." This simply means that before the resurrection, Jesus accomplished all He did with a lesser authority.
4. We are not one with the earthly Christ; we are one with the glorified Christ. Because of our union with Christ, Jesus can now work through us and outdo what He had done before.

Jesus isn't dead, my friend. He is the Head of the Church and we are the Body. We are the hands and feet of the Christ allowing Him to do even greater. Because of union with the glorified Christ, now all glory is ours and all authority in Heaven and on earth is ours!

We must see ourselves for who we are and the works of the earthly Christ for who they are. I don't identify with Jesus of Nazareth; I identify with Jesus of Heaven (1 Corinthians 15:48). We are the fullness of Him that fills all in all (Ephesians 1:23). It is His fullness we have received and grace for grace (John 1:16)!

We must see the greater works as possible and doable… but you can't do greater if the same works seem great. We must renew our mind to Heaven's perspective of who we are and what is possible in Christ. Jesus needs you to believe it and be part of the 8 percent so that He can advance the Church into the greater works through you.

CHAPTER 4
ADVANCE OR DIE

As the Church of Jesus Christ, we must learn from the past. No matter what type of organization it is, whether secular or ministerial, history has shown us repeatedly what happens when you stop advancing: you start dying.

In America, the organizations that continue to thrive over generations are those who continue to advance. A great example of a company that started off with a bang and ended with a fizzle was Blockbuster. Blockbuster was a company that truly seized the idea of video rentals in a great way.

I remember in my late teens and early twenties, at least 1-2 times a week, we were making a trip to Blockbuster to rent a movie. Blockbuster was everywhere! At its peak, Blockbuster had 9,094 stores and employed over 83,000 people all over the world; however, because of poor leadership, Blockbuster didn't advance in insight and revelation of their industry. The leadership of Blockbuster stopped pushing and settled in; as a result, they started dying. By 2010, Blockbuster filed for bankruptcy and in 2014, closed the last remaining company owned stores.

Not only has this happened to scores and scores of secular businesses, we can look at the history of the Church and see it as well. Pretty much every Christian denomination started with a new revelation from God that was built upon a prior revelation; however, give that denomination 10-20 years and do you know what happens? They start dying. As a result of the Azusa Street revival, several denominations were birthed. After 10 years of one of the denominations existence, the great John G. Lake remarked, "After only ten years, the...denomination is already dead."

It is a cycle that has continued on for generations. Why does it happen? Because the new group settles in with their new found revelation and instead of using it to propel themselves forward, they camp where they are at and slowly begin to die. Lester Sumrall once said, "Most Christians never progress past their first revelation of God." Why is that? They think they have it all and as a result, they stop advancing, start settling and start dying. We see this happen with people in their natural lives. The moment people stop becoming active, they start becoming weaker and weaker. In the natural world, if you would simply be active instead of sedentary, we would see less health issues. Why is that? Because even your body needs you to be on the move!

One great minister once said, "You can ride the wave of God all the way to the beach or you can hop on the next wave and the next wave and the next wave." Unfortunately, most ride the wave they started out on and end up on the beach waiting on another move of God; meanwhile, they judge the ones still out on the waves and talk about how they are doing it all wrong!

I am criticized by those who are both older and more experienced than I am, yet they have lost their ambition. Consequently, they disapprove of my efforts to advance. Just because they have lost their backbone, drive, and passion - it doesn't mean I'm going to sit on the beach like a beached whale with them! There are waves to ride, revelations to be gained, and moves of God to initiate and fulfill because there are people that still need to know Him!

When the Church was founded, it began to thrive instantly. Over three thousand people were added to the Church on the first day and another five thousand right after that. Over the last two thousand years, the Church has grown in number, but unfortunately, we have not grown in revelation to the degree that we should have grown.

Some would argue with that statement, but let me show you a scripture that proves we have not really grown like we should.

> Hebrews 6:1-3
> Therefore, leaving the discussion of the elementary *principles* of Christ, let us go on to perfection, not laying again the foundation of repentance from dead works and of faith toward God, of the doctrine of baptisms, of laying on of hands, of resurrection of the dead, and of eternal judgment. And this we will do if God permits.

Look at the subjects that are listed and considered to be 'baby' stuff: repentance, faith, baptism, laying on of hands, resurrection, and judgment. Now, think about what has been preached on for the last hundred years and tell me this: why are we still in elementary school? Certainly, we all need to be reminded of truths and elementary truths must continue to be taught while children are in elementary age - but where are the middle and high school students in Christianity? Where is the growth?

It is interesting that over the last one hundred years, we have heard much about the term *revival*. The word *revival* in regard to religion wasn't really used until the early 1700s. It came to prominence in the 1730s with what is known as the Great Awakening that affected the

English colonies of America. However, in the twentieth century, The Welsh Revival, Azusa Street and the Healing Revival of the 40's and 50's in America occurred and are probably the most well known of the recent past. Regardless of the size and location, the message of those revivals and others mostly consisted of what we see as the elementary principles of Christ - and yet, people act like it's something spectacular.

Revival is a big word in Christendom and we act like it is God giving us something; in reality, revival is God kicking us in the butt and trying to get us to move forward and get where we should have already been! The true revivals of God have been to get us to finish up elementary school and move up a few grades. Why? God wants us to progress!

We look back at our past and in many ways, we glorify these moves of God as something tremendous, but in reality, we should not take these things as a compliment when they happen. Revivals are not the result of God doing something because He is proud of us; God moves in this particular way because the Church as a whole isn't moving — so God has to come into the classroom, wake us up and endeavor to get us moving forward.

Friend, if you are not moving forward, you are moving backward - there is no staying steady in the things of God. Our relationship with God is like a campfire — it is either getting cooler or hotter, but never staying the same. If you are not continually stoking the fire and adding more wood, it is gradually going to get cooler and cooler.

I don't know about you, but I don't want to go backward in the things of God; I want to move forward. I not only want to, but I need to continually be advancing, increasing and multiplying. Too many people are satisfied with fanning the flames by sitting around and talking about the good old days. Well, if I plan on advancing, I can't just fan the flames because they will eventually go out - I need to feed the fire!

How do you feed a natural fire? I have to get up and go get more wood. In the same manner, if I am going to advance in the things of God, I need to go get more fuel for the fire - I need to get more revelation, increase my consciousness of God and then jump into the fire. I don't need to watch the fire burn; I need to burn! I need to burn with a passion for more and more and more and allow the fire of the Holy Spirit to burn through me so that the fire of God burns brighter than it ever has before.

CHAPTER 5
THE FEAR OF LOSING

D.L. Moody said, "Our greatest fear should not be of failure, but of succeeding at something that doesn't really matter."

I would dare say that most people want their life on the earth to count for something. I don't want to be near the end of my life looking back over my life and realizing, "You know what, I didn't do anything that mattered." I not only want to succeed in life, but I want what I succeeded at to actually matter and bring about change in people's lives and the world.

Anyone that knows me knows that I hate losing. I despise losing…I abhor it. I'll be the first to admit: I am a sore loser! I don't care what game we play, I play to win. Even though I play to win, I've never allowed the possibility of losing stop me. I have always enjoyed a challenge.

Growing up, I loved basketball, even though I was usually one of the shorter guys on the court. What I lacked in height, I made up for with hustle, speed, and determination. There were some factors I could not control, but the one thing I could control was how hard I worked. I would do all the dirty stuff most of the others wouldn't do. If the ball was on the floor, I was on the floor. If the ball was going out of bounds, I was jumping into the stands for it. On defense, I would outwork you and frustrate you, and sometimes play a little dirty — whatever was necessary to win!

I never played to lose; I always played to win. Despite my adversity to losing, I never allowed the possibility of losing to be a deterrent. I remember in high school, we were playing against the number one team in the state of Texas and one of the top teams in the country. One of those players went on to the NBA and won several NBA championships.

Needless to say, we were well outmatched and the odds of us winning were pretty much zero; however, I went into the game with the attitude that we could win. I remember being in the locker room and seeing the faces of my teammates right before the game - their faces said it all: we don't have a chance. I gave them a little pep talk about how if we played hard and played perfect, we could win. It seemed to help a bit until the tip off.

I'll never forget standing at half-court of our opponents gym. The referee threw up the ball for the tip off; while the ball was in the air, their small forward took off running from the half-court line towards their rim. The ball was tipped to their point guard who heaved it to their basket for a perfect alley-oop pass to the small forward; this resulted in a thunderous dunk. Their fans went wild, jumping onto the floor in celebration, while all of my teammates hung their heads in defeat. The score was 2-0 and that was about as close as it would get! Thankfully, because of all the commotion from the fans, it gave our coach a minute to gather us together and get my teammates heads back into the game. Our attitudes improved but the final score wasn't pretty. We lost and lost bad. Regardless of the score, and despite losing, I was glad we went in and played hard. I would have rather tried to win than having given up at the beginning. Not only was I our teams leading scorer, I also held one of the best players in the country to one of his lowest scoring games all year (and he was over a foot taller than me!)

It's this attitude I had in sports that I have taken into life. I refuse to allow the fear of losing to stop me from trying. There have been many situations over the last twenty years of ministry in which it looked like there was a great possibility of losing, but in my heart, I knew the Holy Spirit was leading me to do it.

Throughout the Bible, we see various situations in which people stood before impossible situations and moved past the fear of losing by moving into the faith of God. One situation that sticks out to me is that of the Israelites and the evil spies. God had already delivered the Israelites out of the hands of Pharaoh and the Egyptians and had now stated that He had given them the Promised land of Canaan. Moses sent twelve spies into the promised land to come back with a report of the land. Look at their report:

Numbers 13:26-33 NKJV
Now they departed and came back to Moses and Aaron and all the congregation of the children of Israel in the Wilderness of Paran, at Kadesh; they brought back word to them and to all the congregation, and showed them the fruit of the land. Then they told him, and said: "We went to the land where you sent us. It truly flows with milk and honey, and this *is* its fruit. Nevertheless the people who dwell in the land *are* strong; the cities *are* fortified *and* very large; moreover we saw the descendants of Anak there. The Amalekites dwell in the land of the South; the Hittites, the Jebusites, and the Amorites dwell in the mountains; and the Canaanites dwell by the sea and along the banks of the Jordan." Then Caleb quieted the people before Moses, and said, "Let us go up at once and take possession, for

we are well able to overcome it." But the men who had gone up with him said, "We are not able to go up against the people, for they *are* stronger than we." And they gave the children of Israel a bad report of the land which they had spied out, saying, "The land through which we have gone as spies *is* a land that devours its inhabitants, and all the people whom we saw in it *are* men of *great* stature. There we saw the giants (the descendants of Anak came from the giants); and we were like grasshoppers in our own sight, and so we were in their sight."

The spies came back and reported that all God said about the land was true; however, ten of the spies stated it was impossible to take the land because of the fortified cities and the giants.

Because of the evil report of the ten spies, all of Israel gave in to the fear of losing. They were so afraid of losing, they wanted to go back to being a slave in Egypt! Do you see how stupid fear will make you?

Ultimately, this decision cost the Israelites the promise of God and they ended up wandering in the wilderness for forty years until all the doubters died. The fear of losing cost them not only a victory, but ultimately their lives.

You and I will be faced with many situations in life where it will look impossible. There are going to be some situations in which God is going to lead us into so that He can give us some of the things He has promised - but you will have to overcome the fear of losing. The outcome of these situations will not only affect your present but will also affect your future and the futures of people you have never met!

There was another man mentioned in the Bible named David that stood before an impossible situation and in the natural, it was all but settled he would lose. Despite the natural odds against him, he pushed past the fear of losing and pushed into the faith of God.

> 1 Samuel 17:31-51 NKJV
> Now when the words which David spoke were heard, they reported *them* to Saul; and he sent for him. Then David said to Saul, "Let no man's heart fail because of him; your servant will go and fight with this Philistine." And Saul said to David, "You are not able to go against this Philistine to fight with him; for you *are* a youth, and he a man of war from his youth." But David said to Saul, "Your servant used to keep his father's sheep, and when a lion or a bear came and took a lamb out of the flock, I went out after it and struck it, and delivered *the lamb* from its mouth; and when it arose against me, I caught *it*

by its beard, and struck and killed it. Your servant has killed both lion and bear; and this uncircumcised Philistine will be like one of them, seeing he has defied the armies of the living God." Moreover David said, "The LORD, who delivered me from the paw of the lion and from the paw of the bear, He will deliver me from the hand of this Philistine." And Saul said to David, "Go, and the LORD be with you!" So Saul clothed David with his armor, and he put a bronze helmet on his head; he also clothed him with a coat of mail. David fastened his sword to his armor and tried to walk, for he had not tested *them.* And David said to Saul, "I cannot walk with these, for I have not tested *them.*" So David took them off. Then he took his staff in his hand; and he chose for himself five smooth stones from the brook, and put them in a shepherd's bag, in a pouch which he had, and his sling was in his hand. And he drew near to the Philistine. So the Philistine came, and began drawing near to David, and the man who bore the shield *went* before him. And when the Philistine looked about and saw David, he disdained him; for he was *only* a youth, ruddy and good-looking. So the Philistine said to David, "*Am* I a dog, that you come to me with sticks?" And the Philistine cursed David by his gods. And the Philistine said to David, "Come to me, and I will give your flesh to the birds of the air and the beasts of the field!" Then David said to the Philistine, "You come to me with a sword, with a spear, and with a javelin. But I come to you in the name of the LORD of hosts, the God of the armies of Israel, whom you have defied. This day the LORD will deliver you into my hand, and I will strike you and take your head from you. And this day I will give the carcasses of the camp of the Philistines to the birds of the air and the wild beasts of the earth, that all the earth may know that there is a God in Israel. Then all this assembly shall know that the LORD does not save with sword and spear; for the battle *is* the LORD's, and He will give you into our hands."So it was, when the Philistine arose and came and drew near to meet David, that David hurried and ran toward the army to meet the Philistine. Then David put his hand in his bag and took out a stone; and he slung *it and* struck the Philistine in his forehead, so that the stone sank into his forehead, and he fell on his face to the earth. So David prevailed over the Philistine with a sling and a stone, and struck the Philistine and killed him. But *there was* no sword in the hand of David. Therefore David ran and stood over the Philistine, took his sword and drew it out of its sheath and killed him, and cut off his head with it.

David was told it was impossible and that he would lose, but that did not stop David from moving forward. David walked away from impossibilities and ran toward what was possible, but also what was doable: kill the giant and deliver his people. Because of David's attitude and the resulting actions, all of Israel was delivered. You don't run from the giant; you run toward the giant. Always remember: you never run from a lion; you become the lion!

Several years ago, I was faced with a decision that could have had horrible repercussions if it went wrong. I had been sensing it was time to start putting my full focus on the healing ministry—which meant I needed to step down from my pastoral position of the church Lacy and I had started and begin traveling full time. Many people look at where things are at presently and would think that decision was not a big deal, but it was a huge deal because I didn't have ministry partners and I had no schedule. On top of that, I had made a decision that if this was what God was calling me to do, there were three things I was not going to do: (1) I would never ask for meetings from pastors (2) I would never make any financial demands and (3) I would cover all of my travel costs. As you can see, the odds were already stacked against me!

Well, Lacy and I sensed it was the right thing to do, so we met with our team and made an announcement at our church. We moved to Oklahoma and do you know what happened a few months later? Covid showed up and all travel was shut down and most churches closed. Now, can you imagine what was going through my mind at that point? Well, Lacy came up to me one day and told me exactly what I was thinking but I wasn't saying! She said, "Chad, I know we are doing what God told us to do, but on paper, we look like fools. You have one meeting for the entire year, a handful of partners, we have no jobs and you are starting a traveling ministry focused on healing in the middle of a worldwide pandemic…and you are not asking for meetings." We both couldn't help but laugh because when you heard it audibly, it sounded even more ridiculous outside of my head than it did in my head!

Right there in my office, we both got over the fear of losing and went all in. I didn't know how, but I just knew God was going to open the doors.

One Sunday morning, I had an older gentleman come up to me at the end of the service. He said, "Chad, I have a word from the Lord for you. The Lord showed me that its like you have been flying at 50,000 feet for several years. During this time, God has been showing you things other people haven't seen, but He is about to create a runway for you to land on and tell the world about these hidden things of God."

Now I will be honest, when a stranger comes up to me and says they have a word from the Lord for me, I take it with a great deal of skepticism...but there was something different about this situation: it bore witness with me. I had never met this man before, but I knew God was up to something.

A few weeks later, I received a call from a major Christian television ministry and from that, the ministry doors blew open. The letters and emails from pastors and new partners started coming in.

Soon, the letters and emails started coming in from pastors and new partners. At the end of 2020, we ended up having our best year ministerially and financially we had ever had. Do you know what happened in 2021? We doubled what we did in 2020! Do you know what has happened every year since then? We have doubled in number every year! Friends, that is the faithfulness of God! When you get over the fear of losing, you get into the grace of God where all things are not only possible, they are doable. As the result of what was the craziest decision (in the natural) of my entire adult life, we have seen countless miracles and lives changed all over the world. Friend, God is faithful. Get over the fear of losing and get into the place of advancing.

CHAPTER 6
THE WORLD IS DEPENDING ON YOU

It is easy to get to a place of settling when you are only focused on yourself. When things are going good for you, there is a tendency to stop pushing; however, when you realize that what you are doing is for the greater good of others, it will push you to go further.

After graduating Bible school at twenty-six years old, I began working on my masters degree in counseling. At the same time, I was working for the state of Texas as a counselor. One day I was sitting in my office and was reading my Bible during a break. I will never forget that day that the Lord spoke so clearly to me; it was almost as if someone was standing right beside me. He said, "You need to get strong in the area of healing." From that day on, I began studying and asking for more revelation and insight because I realized it was about more than just me.

Over the years, I have received criticism from people, especially ministers, as I have continued to push for greater. I have never been one to settle for average, but when it comes to your life calling, why would you not continually be pushing the boundaries when you know there is more available?

The other day, I saw an interview from the 1980s about the use of debit cards in restaurants. People were being critical about the idea of using a card instead of cash; one business man stated, "It seems like a waste of time to me; I don't ever see cards being used in restaurants instead of cash." Well, looking back, that business man must feel pretty stupid at such a small minded statement. But you see, these types of criticisms come from every area of life and business…as well as ministry.

In the area of healing, I get criticized royally for my stance and my teaching; however, it is easy to criticize when it doesn't affect you on a day to day basis. I have people travel from great distances to my meetings in search of hope and a cure for their physical ailment; although I am not the healer, I put tremendous pressure on myself to advance, increase and multiply in my understanding and results in the area of healing. Why do I put this pressure on myself? For two reasons: (1) people's physical lives are on the line and (2) people's spiritual lives are on the line.

There are multitudes of Christians who are in dire need of healing and they are looking for help. Although Jesus has already provided healing for every believer, many people still need help in making that connection and that is where I, along with others, must step up and connect them to God. God is so gracious in that He has provided several avenues for His healing power to get into the body. When we look at the current state of the body of Christ and compare it to the realities we see in the Word, it's glaringly obvious we have work to do in getting our results up to the standard of Jesus Christ. How does it happen? We humble ourselves and recognize where we are at and then push for more revelation and understanding so that we can help people.

Outside of Christians, there are hundreds of millions of unbelievers who are in need of healing for their bodies. For them to experience God's power, it requires sons and daughters of God to release it to them — and this is part of the Great Commission. It's vital that we advance and grow in the area of healing so that the sinner can receive healing and allow that sign of God to open their heart so they can receive the good news of Jesus Christ.

We owe the world an encounter with God. We owe the world God's healing power. We owe them the opportunity to experience the goodness of God. It is because of this, I refuse to settle for the religious excuses of our day. It is because of people I have never met, that I continue to push for more revelation. It is because of people that are hurting, dying and looking for hope that I push everyday for continued insight and advancement in the things of God. There are people I haven't met yet that are counting on me to get to a place of understanding so that they can experience the freedom that only Jesus can give. The world doesn't need more advancement from Silicon Valley, but they do need more advancement from the Church. The world is depending on you to advance so that they can be truly free.

CHAPTER 7
STORMS AND PHARISEES

If you are going to advance, there are two things you are going to encounter: storms and Pharisees. When you look at the life of Jesus, you find that satan was using various ways to try and stop Him from bringing increase and advancement.

> Luke 8:22-26 NKJV
> Now it happened, on a certain day, that He got into a boat with His disciples. And He said to them, "Let us cross over to the other side of the lake." And they launched out. But as they sailed He fell asleep. And a windstorm came down on the lake, and they were filling *with water,* and were in jeopardy. And they came to Him and awoke Him, saying, "Master, Master, we are perishing!" Then He arose and rebuked the wind and the raging of the water. And they ceased,

and there was a calm. But He said to them, "Where is your faith?" And they were afraid, and marveled, saying to one another, "Who can this be? For He commands even the winds and water, and they obey Him!" Then they sailed to the country of the Gadarenes, which is opposite Galilee. And when He stepped out on the land, there met Him a certain man from the city who had demons for a long time. And he wore no clothes, nor did he live in a house but in the tombs.

The story of Jesus calming the storm is a familiar story to many people, but I don't think we truly have understood the full story. Several of these disciples were professional fishermen; they knew the waters and they knew the weather. The Sea of Galilee is a massive lake roughly 7 miles (11 kilometers) wide and roughly 12 miles (21 kilometers) from north to south; they would not have gone out into the water with a storm brewing.

Notice the Bible says that a windstorm came down on the lake. This was a demonic storm; a storm the disciples were not expecting and that took them by surprise. This was a storm they could feel but could not see: a great storm of wind — opposition that was coming to stop them. Now, we often focus on Jesus stopping the storm, but have you ever stopped to think why the storm came? It was because Jesus was heading to the country of the Gadarenes. What was in this country? The madman of Gadera who, through the legion of demons possessing him, was making this part of the country impassable and unreachable.

Jesus' entire purpose in crossing the Sea of Galilee was to go to the Gadarenes and set the demon possessed man free. This ministry trip was not only going to set this man free, but also set the region free! You will find that many times, when you are on the brink of a breakthrough, that is when satan will try to stop you. When you step out to advance and take new territory, it should not surprise you that satan will bring out all the stops to hinder you from expanding the kingdom of God. Friend, many times you will hear people say that the reason people are experiencing the storms of life is because they are out of the will of God - but that is not always the case. In reality, if you are in the will of God, it is guaranteed storms will come to not only hinder you, but take you out completely.

At the point of our ministry beginning to take some serious ground for the kingdom of God, when we had the greatest momentum and experiencing some of the greatest miracles, I had the worst storm of life one could ever experience: my sweet Lacy moved to Heaven. We were about to experience our twentieth wedding anniversary and while Jake and I were on a ministry trip in Dallas, Texas, satan took her life. It was totally unexpected and devastating.

That moment will forever be etched in my soul. I will never forget sitting at our gate at DFW airport. After a weekend of ministry, Jake and I were waiting to board our flight home. Lacy called me and told me she couldn't feel her legs or hands and her tongue was starting to go numb. I told Lacy I would call her right back, hung up and immediately called 911 and told them the situation. I then called Lacy back and told her 911 was on the way. As I was talking to her, she stopped responding to me. I hung up and called back several times with no answer.

It was at that point, the Delta agent came over the loud speaker and announced it was time to board our flight. As I am getting on the flight, I am frantically calling 911 trying to get any information that I could; but because of HIPPA laws, all they would tell me was that they were on the scene.

One can only try to imagine the thoughts that were running through my mind and the fears trying to grip hold of me while I sat there praying in tongues.

After being in the air for about an hour, I received a call on my cell from the Hillsborough County Sheriff. He said, "Mr. Gonzales, we don't typically do this, but I have been told of the situation that you and your son are on a flight heading this way and so I wanted to call and personally tell you so you were not sitting on a 3 hour flight not knowing anything. I hate telling you this, but I wanted you to know that when the paramedics arrived, Lacy was unresponsive and had been gone for probably twenty minutes before we arrived. We did everything we could."

I will never forget that moment. With my Jake sitting to my right, not knowing that anything was wrong, I had a choice to make: quit or keep pushing. Well, it took half a second—not only do I keep pushing, I'm going to push even harder.

I took this personally because I knew this was an attack on me. Satan goes about like a roaring lion seeking whom he may devour. He couldn't get me, so he went after my Lacy.

I sat on that flight for the next two hours fighting every second to maintain my thoughts, keep my emotions under control, and pray in the spirit for the wisdom, strength and words to not only tell Jake that his mother was in Heaven, but also figure out how to move forward.

Not many people knew, but Lacy, with her big smile and vibrant personality, had been silently struggling with anxiety for years. This included a deep-seated fear of dying young and not being there for our son, Jake. Her anxiety had grown to such an extent that even Jake felt its impact, leading him to fear falling asleep with thoughts of his own mortality.

Thankfully, in her last year, she courageously started to overcome these challenges. The prolonged period of this anxiety created vulnerabilities that satan took full advantage of. Unbeknownst to all of us, including Lacy, a tumor had been growing on her colon for about 3-4 years. It was only during her autopsy that we learned this tumor had caused a rupture in her small intestine, leading to septic shock.

The memory of sitting in the parking garage of the Tampa airport at 2:30am on April 3rd, 2023, remains vivid in my mind. I'd held it together all the way through the airport and to the car, but now I had to tell Jake that Lacy wouldn't be at home to greet us. We sat in my Jeep, holding each other and crying so hard that sound stops coming out of your mouth. It was a hurt that I didn't know was even possible for myself and even more so for my son.

After we got our emotions under control, Jake, being 14 years-old, looked at me and made one of the most mind blowing statements. Jake said, "Dad, I know you won't let satan do anything to you and I know you won't let satan do anything to me, but you couldn't control mom's thoughts." I sat on the driver's side of my Jeep completely stunned that in the intensity of the moment, Jake had the spiritual insight and fortitude to recognize and understand these things, especially at his age. I looked at him and said, "Jake, we are going to learn from this and you and me, we're going to finish what me and your mother started."

Friend, know this right now: it is never God's will for His children to die young. Certainly, it is better to be with the Lord than to be in this flesh, but there is also a plan God has for us to fulfill…and you don't fulfill it in only forty years of age. Although it wasn't the will of God for Lacy to move to Heaven so early, I knew it was the will of God for me to continue moving forward. Why? Because ultimately, it is about the Kingdom of God and finishing what God has called us to do.

You must know that when you decide to advance and go after greater, there will be attacks. Why is that? Because you have an enemy that does not want to give up territory. Satan may not use a physical storm to stop you, but he will use life situations and various circumstances to hinder, oppose and discourage you from moving forward. God is depending on you and I to expand His kingdom, but you and I must be prepared beforehand to know that the storms will come — and when they do, instead of being discouraged, we recognize who is behind the storms, take authority over them and keep going forward.

When we are going after greater, not only will we experience the storms of life, we will experience the Pharisees. What are the Pharisees? In Jesus' time on the earth, the

Pharisees were the religious leaders of the day. They knew all of the Old Testament scripture but they were so intelligent with it, they stripped it of its power. They would be those that could teach videos about a subject, write books about the subject, lecture on the subject, tell you the history of the subject and yet be satisfied with producing no fruit on the subject. Not only were they extremely intellectual, they were also extremely critical. Now friend, I've got bad news for you: we still have Pharisees today. They certainly have more revelation than those in Jesus' day, but they are still here today to be your greatest critic.

I am telling you right now, you better get ready for the critics. A lot of people don't like it when you push for more. Do you know why? Because it exposes their lack of desire to increase and/or exposes their inefficiencies. Pharisees love talking, but don't care about producing. Jesus even warned his disciples about the Pharisees.

> Luke 12:1
> In the meantime, when an innumerable multitude of people had gathered together, so that they trampled one another, He began to say to His disciples first *of all,* "Beware of the leaven of the Pharisees, which is hypocrisy.

The leaven or you could say mindset of the Pharisees was that God was at the center of everything and yet, in their mindset, powerless to change anything. It was an issue 2,000 years ago and yet it is a greater issue today. Do you know why? Because we are some of the most learned Christians who have ever lived. Knowledge is great as long as you keep advancing, but the moment you stop advancing, you start dying — and criticizing those who are still endeavoring to live.

Over the years, I have had my fair share of critics, but those critics didn't come out until I started down a new, narrow road. I have found that when you are on the wide road, that is the popular road full of cheerleaders — it is a road that doesn't lead to growth, but simply designed to keep you moving. As soon as you start endeavoring to create a new road, the critics will be in the ditches to tell you how you are wrong. I love people, but I do not care about people's opinions about me... good or bad. If you live by people's praise, you'll die by their criticism.

People's words do not move me. Do you know what moves me? What moves me and keeps me advancing is to finish the work of what Jesus has called me to do.

> Hebrews 12:1-4
> Therefore we also, since we are surrounded by so great a cloud of witnesses, let us lay aside every weight, and the sin which so easily ensnares *us,* and let us run with endurance the race that is set before us, looking unto Jesus, the

author and finisher of *our* faith, who for the joy that was set before Him endured the cross, despising the shame, and has sat down at the right hand of the throne of God. For consider Him who endured such hostility from sinners against Himself, lest you become weary and discouraged in your souls. You have not yet resisted to bloodshed, striving against sin.

You will find that Jesus was solely focused on one thing: finishing the work God sent Him to do. Despite the shame and the persecution, Jesus kept going because He had His eyes on the prize. Ultimately, it was the Pharisees who had Jesus killed. They were scheming behind the scenes looking for ways to get rid of Him. Even though Jesus always walked in love, He always told the truth…even when it came to who the Pharisees really were:

Matthew 23:1-3,13, 16-17, 27-28, 32-33
Then Jesus spoke to the multitudes and to His disciples, saying: "The scribes and the Pharisees sit in Moses' seat. Therefore whatever they tell you to observe, *that* observe and do, but do not do according to their works; for they say, and do not do."
"But woe to you, scribes and Pharisees, hypocrites! For you shut up the kingdom of heaven against men; for you neither go in *your-*

selves, nor do you allow those who are entering to go in.

"Woe to you, blind guides, who say, 'Whoever swears by the temple, it is nothing; but whoever swears by the gold of the temple, he is obliged *to perform it.*' Fools and blind! For which is greater, the gold or the temple that sanctifies the gold?

"Woe to you, scribes and Pharisees, hypocrites! For you are like whitewashed tombs which indeed appear beautiful outwardly, but inside are full of dead *men's* bones and all uncleanness. Even so you also outwardly appear righteous to men, but inside you are full of hypocrisy and lawlessness.

Fill up, then, the measure of your fathers' *guilt.* Serpents, brood of vipers! How can you escape the condemnation of hell?

In Matthew 23, Jesus didn't hold back in his observation of the Pharisees. He called them:

1. Hypocrites
2. Fools
3. Blind guides
4. Whitewashed tombs filled with uncleanness
5. Brood of vipers

Obviously, Jesus didn't think highly of them; He even said, "How can you escape the condemnation of Hell?" This certainly isn't the Jesus we hear preached today, but it is the real Jesus. Friend, just because you know Scripture doesn't mean you know God.

Now I certainly believe that the vast majority of Christians are good hearted and love the Lord, but most people do not like change or to be challenged. Have you ever heard the phrase, "You can't teach an old dog new tricks?" Well, it's not that you can't; it's that an old dog doesn't really care about learning any new tricks!

I've found it odd that most of the criticism I receive comes from those older than me; rarely is it coming from those my age or younger. Why is that? Because progress means change.

I know even when it comes to small cities, I have known of a few small towns that didn't want growth and have angrily fought against any large business or development that tries to come through. As odd as it may sound, I even know of churches that do not want growth because they are satisfied with their little group and want to keep it that way.

As much as people resist change and criticize those pushing for change, we must be the catalysts for change…not for the sake of change, but for the sake of advancement. The more you push, the more criticism will come - but that is okay! If Jesus dealt with Pharisees, you and I will deal with Pharisees. It is going to take skin made of steel, a heart full of love and forgiveness and a focus that is so singular and determined, nothing will be able to deter you.

When you listen to the words of Jesus, you find that His eyes were fixed on finishing what He started.

> John 4:34
> Jesus said to them, "My food is to do the will of Him who sent Me, and to finish His work.

> John 5:36
> But I have a greater witness than John's; for the works which the Father has given Me to finish—the very works that I do—bear witness of Me, that the Father has sent Me.

> John 17:4
> I have glorified You on the earth. I have finished the work which You have given Me to do.

Notice that finishing the work God sent Him to do was the driving factor in His life. "My food is to do the will of Him who sent Me and to finish His work." The mission was what sustained Him and drove Him. I am the same way. In spite of being slandered in the media, unlawful legal attacks, church splits, physical threats, loss of relationships and even the loss of my late wife Lacy, I have not allowed any of it to cause me to slow down or even question for a moment the will of God for my life. I am about as stubborn as it gets; when I make up my mind to do something, you better believe nothing will stop me. All of the storms and Pharisees in my life have done one thing: poured gasoline on the fire burning within me to complete what God has called me to do.

In my last hours on the Earth, my goal is to stand before Jesus and confidently say, "I have glorified You on the earth. I have finished the work which You have given me to do."

CHAPTER 8
PROTECT THE DREAM

Every one of us have a dream that needs to be fulfilled, but in order to fulfill it, we must protect it. One great example of this in the Bible is found in the story of Joseph.

> Genesis 37
> Now Jacob dwelt in the land where his father was a stranger, in the land of Canaan. This *is* the history of Jacob. Joseph, *being* seventeen years old, was feeding the flock with his brothers. And the lad *was* with the sons of Bilhah and the sons of Zilpah, his father's wives; and Joseph brought a bad report of them to his father. Now Israel loved Joseph more than all his children, because he *was* the son of his old age. Also he made him a tunic of *many* colors. But when his brothers saw that their father loved him more than all his

brothers, they hated him and could not speak peaceably to him. Now Joseph had a dream, and he told *it* to his brothers; and they hated him even more. So he said to them, "Please hear this dream which I have dreamed: There we were, binding sheaves in the field. Then behold, my sheaf arose and also stood upright; and indeed your sheaves stood all around and bowed down to my sheaf." And his brothers said to him, "Shall you indeed reign over us? Or shall you indeed have dominion over us?" So they hated him even more for his dreams and for his words. Then he dreamed still another dream and told it to his brothers, and said, "Look, I have dreamed another dream. And this time, the sun, the moon, and the eleven stars bowed down to me." So he told *it* to his father and his brothers; and his father rebuked him and said to him, "What *is* this dream that you have dreamed? Shall your mother and I and your brothers indeed come to bow down to the earth before you?" 11 And his brothers envied him, but his father kept the matter *in mind.*

Joseph was given dreams to reveal things about his future. Instead of keeping them to himself, he told those dreams to his family and it led to years of hell. His brothers despised him so much, they dug a pit, threw Joseph in it and left him for dead. Because of the "kindness" of one brother, they decided to pull Joseph out of the pit and sell him as a slave. Joseph eventually ends up serving in Potiphar's house - only to be accused of rape and then thrown in prison. Eventually, because of the favor of God, Joseph interprets a dream for Pharaoh and is promoted to second in command of Egypt. It's a wild story of how Joseph became the prince of Egypt, but I have often wondered, "Did Joseph really have to be left for dead, become a slave, be accused of rape and thrown in prison…just so God could get him before Pharaoh?" Most people say this entire process was the plan of God, but I'm not so sure about that.

Have you ever heard the statement, "Don't cast your pearls before swine?"

> Matthew 7:6 NKJV
> Do not give what is holy to the dogs; nor cast your pearls before swine, lest they trample them under their feet, and turn and tear you in pieces.

Jesus is the one who said this and it is an extremely wise statement. When it comes to Joseph, I often think of this statement by Jesus. What would have happened if Joseph would have kept those dreams to himself? Joseph's brothers already hated him because of the favoritism shown to him by his father. Instead of using some wisdom and keeping the dream to himself, Joseph told his extremely jealous brothers that one day, they would bow down and serve him. Where was the wisdom in that? Think about the statement of Jesus in relation to Joseph: "Don't cast your pearls before swine, for they will trample you under their feet and tear you to pieces."

What would have happened if he would have just put the dream on the shelf of his mind, meditated, prayed about it and allowed God to bring it to pass? Yes, God is sovereign and can fulfill His plans however He chooses, however, I firmly believe if Joseph would have been wise about the revealing of his dreams, he wouldn't have had to go through all of that torment in order for those dreams to come to pass.

Isn't it interesting that Jesus didn't go around telling everyone everything that God had put in His heart? How many times would Jesus tell people not to reveal who He was or not to tell what had happened? There was wisdom and purpose in that so that Jesus would not have unnecessary hindrances to fulfilling the plan of God. Just because God has shown you something for your future, it doesn't mean you need to just start blabbing it to all those around you. God wants you to go for greater and that is why He will give you thoughts, ideas and insight into your future. He will give you glimpses and knowings of the things He has for you, but you would be a fool to just start going out and telling everyone.

There are things God showed me decades ago and I never told anyone. Instead of announcing to my family, friends and the entire world on social media, I have kept these precious pearls to myself. If Joseph were alive today, he probably would have woken up from his dream and done a live stream on Facebook and Instagram to tell everyone about it. I watch so many people do this and I just can't understand it — there are some dreams God has given you that you need to allow to take root in you, grow in you and develop in you before you go out and start talking about it. Even the Apostle Paul spent three years away from everyone before he approached the Apostle Peter about what Jesus had revealed to him!

> Galatians 1:15-18
> But when God, who set me apart from my mother's womb and called me by his grace, was pleased 16 to reveal his Son in me so that I might preach him among the Gentiles, my immediate response was not to consult any human being. I did not go up to Jerusalem to see those who were apostles before I was, but I went into Arabia. Later I returned to Damascus. Then after three years, I went up to Jerusalem to get acquainted with Cephas and stayed with him fifteen days.

Friend, you have to understand that know one sees the potential in you like God. People around you may love you, but the majority will also judge you because they know your past and your shortcomings. Familiarity breeds contempt — even when the dream is amazing. Unfortunately, some of your biggest critics will be of the same bloodline.

There are also things I am just not interested in announcing so that satan can get a jumpstart in trying to stop the dream. People act like satan is all knowing, but that is not the case. I can show you time after time in my life in which everything was fine until I announced God's next plan...and then all of a sudden, all hell began to break loose in my life to try and stop the dream. The moment satan finds out what God is endeavoring to do through you, he will jump into action to try and stop the Word from coming to pass.

> Mark 4:13-17 NKJV
> And He said to them, "Do you not understand this parable? How then will you understand all the parables? The sower sows the word. And these are the ones by the wayside where the word is sown. When they hear, Satan comes immediately and takes away the word that was sown in their hearts. These likewise are the ones sown on stony ground who, when they hear the word, immediately receive it with gladness; and

they have no root in themselves, and so endure only for a time. Afterward, when tribulation or persecution arises for the word's sake, immediately they stumble.

Ultimately, you will find that few people around you are dream makers but most people around you are dream killers. Satan can't stop you, but he will influence carnal Christians to give you outright criticism or doubt that is dressed in wisdom. I can't tell you how many times I have had people, even ministers, tell me, "Now Chad, you need to use wisdom." It wasn't wisdom they wanted me to use; it was their unbelief they wanted me to use.

Just because someone is spirit-filled doesn't mean they are being spirit led! They may be giving advice from a good heart, but that doesn't mean their advice is rooted in the dream God gave you. I am all for wise counsel, but I have wholly followed something I heard Oral Roberts say many years ago: "Once you have heard from God, confer with man no more."

The dreams God gives you are usually bigger than what most people can handle. If I told people some of the things God has shown me, some would tell me I was conceited, others would tell me it's just not possible and others would just flat out be offended. So do you know what I have done with all of these God plans and dreams? I have hidden them in my heart, meditated on them and over time, I have watched God bring them to pass.

I don't need to share my dreams with everyone; especially those who don't share my vision and can't help in bringing it to pass. The only one who can bring the dream to pass is God! I would rather God bring the dream to pass instead of me looking to others to bring the dream to pass. I know full well that it will take people to make the dream come to fruition, but God knows exactly who those people are and He will speak to them. It is not my job to put pressure on people and look to them to bring the dream to pass. My job is simple: do what God has called me to do and He will do the rest. God authors the dreams and He will finish them.

CHAPTER 9
HARNESS YOUR IMAGINATION

In Genesis 11, we find the story about the Tower of Babel. At that point in history, all of the people of the earth had not spread out; it is widely believed that all of civilization was in what we know as modern Iraq. The Bible says they all had one language and they had determined to build a tower that would reach to Heaven.

> Genesis 11:6 KJV
> And the LORD said, Behold, the people is one, and they have all one language; and this they begin to do: and now nothing will be restrained from them, which they have imagined to do.

In teaching about this passage of scripture, most people use the story of the tower of Babel to talk about leadership and unity - but we miss out on the most important piece. Notice the last phrase of this verse: "...and now nothing will be restrained from them which they have imagined to do." All of this started with their imagination! God gave you an imagination and you will find that this is where vision and dreams are birthed.

The Bible talks much about our imagination and yet we rarely hear anything about it in church. When we do hear about it, the imagination is usually talked about in a negative sense - but God gave it to us! In Ephesians, the apostle Paul actually prays that our imagination would be filled with the insight and understanding of God!

Ephesians 1:15-20 NKJV
Therefore I also, after I heard of your faith in the Lord Jesus and your love for all the saints, do not cease to give thanks for you, making mention of you in my prayers: that the God of our Lord Jesus Christ, the Father of glory, may give to you the spirit of wisdom and revelation in the knowledge of Him, the eyes of your understanding being enlightened; that you may know what is the hope of His calling, what are the riches of the glory of His inheritance in the saints, and what *is* the exceeding greatness of His power toward us who believe, according to the working of His mighty power which He worked in Christ when He raised Him from the dead and seated *Him* at His right hand in the heavenly *places,*

The Apostle Paul prays that the eyes of our understanding would be filled with the light of God's wisdom and revelation. The word *understanding* in verse 18 is the Greek word *Dianoia* which literally means "the mind as a faculty of understanding, feeling, desiring" and is translated as *imagination*.[1]

God wants you to use your imagination for His good! We are great at using our imagination - we just usually use it for the curse. People are great at imagining the worst possible scenarios of bad news. I have literally watched people extremely close to me imagine themselves into sickness because they were constantly allowing their thought life to think about it and be worried about it. Do you realize that worry is simply you allowing your imagination to run wild with thoughts of doubt and fear? Worrying is simply meditation used for evil instead of meditation or imagination used for good!

> Joshua 1:8 NKJV
> This Book of the Law shall not depart from your mouth, but you shall meditate in it day and night, that you may observe to do according to all that is written in it. For then you will make your way prosperous, and then you will have good success.

The word *meditate* in Joshua 1:8 is the Hebrew word *Hagah*. Take a wild guess at what it means? Not only does it mean to muse, mutter, meditate, devise, and plot, it also means imagine.[2]

God's instructions to Joshua was to take His Word and fill His imagination with it and then let His imagination run wild all throughout the day with the Word of God. What would be the result? Joshua would know what needed to be done and he would be successful in doing it.

Notice God didn't instruct Joshua to call a meeting before all of the Israelites and tell them all of God's secrets to him. Today most people would be tempted to quickly post a video on social media to announce the big plans - but that isn't what God told Joshua to do. One of the most spiritual and beneficial things you can do is to spend time imagining the dreams God has for you.

If you are like me, I don't like to sit still - I feel like I need to be doing something. For many years, I felt like I needed to be doing something with my hands in order to accomplish something for the day; however, I found I can accomplish great things with my imagination as well.

These days, you will find me spending a lot of time just sitting and imagining. I allow my mind to just wander the trails of God and see what He has for me. Why would I do that? Because I have the mind of Christ! Now certainly just sitting around and imagining isn't going to get the job done. Notice God told Joshua to meditate day and night on the word so he would know what to do. There is imagining which leads to doing - but it's my imagining that leads to the life of God which will cause the doing to be successful.

> Ephesians 4:17-18 NKJV
> This I say, therefore, and testify in the Lord, that you should no longer walk as the rest of the Gentiles walk, in the futility of their mind, having their understanding darkened, being alienated from the life of God, because of the ignorance that is in them, because of the blindness of their heart;

Look at God's command: don't be like the Gentiles in the futility of their mind, having their understanding darkened, being alienated from the life of God. The word understanding is the same Greek word meaning *imagination* that is also found in Ephesians 1:18. Their imaginations are darkened, alienating them from the life of God. When your imagination is filled with the light of God, it will lead to the life of God flowing in your life and situation.

Friend, you need to take the dream God has given you and daily, spend time imagining it. Do you know what that will do? It will give you the image God wants you to focus on so that you (1) know what you are working toward and (2) know how to do it. The more you can see it, the more it will become part of you and the more it becomes part of you, no amount of criticism or hard times will be able to stop you.

Never has there been someone who has advanced and gone after greater without imagining first. Why?

1. You will never blaze new trails without first seeing it in your imagination. Your imagination is where the vision is birthed.
2. You will never accomplish the impossible without seeing the possible in your imagination. There is no faith where there is no hope and your imagination is the factory in which hope is produced.
3. You'll never hold to the vision until the vision becomes part of you. People may talk you out of a possession but they can't talk you out of your identity.

God needs you to advance, to increase and to multiply. He needs you to go after greater and so does the world. One year from now, you should be able to look back to this day and see that there has been an increase in the area in which God has called you. The imagination is one of the greatest tools God has given you to tap into the Kingdom of God and walk out its realities in this world. Whatever has your imagination will have your faith and whatever has your faith is what will be produced in your life. If you want to go after greater in your life, you will first have to go after greater in your imagination.

ABOUT THE AUTHOR

Chad Gonzales is a passionate visionary with a mission to elevate the Church to the standard set by Jesus Himself. His heart's desire is for believers to awaken to their true identity in Christ and manifest Heaven on Earth as children of God. With a strong emphasis on identity in Christ and the ministry of healing, Chad fearlessly declares the Word of God, resulting in frequent miraculous healings in his ministry, including restored sight, hearing, and even the dissolution of tumors.

As the founder of The Healing Academy, Chad has devoted his life to helping individuals unlock their divine potential and experience the supernatural. His extensive educational background includes a Master of Education in Counseling from Lamar University and a Doctorate of Ministry from the School of Bible Theology Seminary and University, equipping him with a profound understanding of the human mind and spirit.

With over two decades of pastoral and church-planting experience, Chad intimately understands the needs and struggles of believers, providing practical guidance and support. He is also a prolific author, known for empowering believers with books like "The Supernatural Prayer of Jesus: Secrets from the Son of God That Unleash The Miracle Realm."

Based in vibrant Tampa, Florida, Chad serves as the driving force behind Chad Gonzales Ministries, where he continues to write captivating books and contributes to the development of Union University, an innovative online Bible school designed to offer comprehensive spiritual education worldwide.

Through his teachings, programs, and media platforms such as The Way Of Life television program and The Supernatural Life Podcast, Chad has left an indelible mark on the lives of thousands both nationally and internationally. He is a living testament to the miraculous power of faith and the boundless possibilities that await those who dare to believe.

To learn more about Chad Gonzales and his ministry, visit www.chadgonzales.com. Join him on a journey to embrace the supernatural and walk in the footsteps of Jesus.

ALSO BY CHAD GONZALES

Advance

Aliens

An Alternate Reality

Believing God For A House

Eight Percent

Fearless

God's Will Is You Healed

Making Right Decisions

Naturally Supernatural

Possessors of Life

The Supernatural Prayer of Jesus

Think Like Jesus

Walking In The Miraculous

THE SUPERNATURAL LIFE PODCAST

Check out *The Supernatural Life Podcast* with Chad Gonzales! New episodes are available each month designed to help you connect with God on a deeper level and live the supernatural life God desires for you to have.

THE HEALING ACADEMY

The Healing Academy is an outreach of Chad Gonzales Ministries to help the everyday believer learn to walk according to the standard of Jesus in the ministry of healing.

Jesus said in John 14:12 that whoever believes in Him would do the same works and even greater works. Through The Healing Academy, it is our goal to raise the standard of the healing ministry in the Church and manifest the ministry of Jesus in the marketplace.

The Healing Academy is available online as well as in person training. For more information, please visit thehealingacademy.com

MORE FROM CGM

Looking to attend a Live event with Chad? Visit chadgonzales.com/schedule or scan the QR code to find an event near you.

NOTES

2. GREATER IS ALWAYS POSSIBLE

1. https://www.biblestudytools.com/lexicons/greek/kjv/rhema.html

9. HARNESS YOUR IMAGINATION

1. (https://www.biblestudytools.com/lexicons/greek/kjv/dianoia.html)
2. (https://www.biblestudytools.com/lexicons/hebrew/kjv/hagah.html)